Progressive Frequency

By Sheryl Rodriguez

@soul_twerker

That Guy's House

Copyright © 2019, Sheryl Rodriguez

All rights reserved. No part of this publication may be reproduced, distributed or transmitted in any form or by any means without permission of the publisher, except in the case of brief quotations referencing the body of work and in accordance with copyright law.

ISBN - 978-1-912779-80-2 (print)

ISBN - 978-1-912779-81-9 (ebook)

Book Design by Michael Maloney

First edition published in 2019

That Guy's House

20-22 Wenlock Road

London

England

N1 7GU

www.ThatGuysHouse.com

This book is dedicated to my daughter Rachel.

My beacon of light, vessel of love.

My up when everything is down, right when everything is left, glow when everything is dark. I am infinitely grateful to walk through life with you.

When another being gave me hope after I couldn't find any, I knew angels were real. Your soul was chosen to encounter mine. You have taken everything I taught you and blossomed into an amazing prodigy. Your intuitive ways always catch me off guard but you keep me on my toes and fill me with purpose. Your spirit lights up energies that have been deprived of love. I won't fight your growth in this world by introducing you to the curse of conforming. Your purpose was to remind me that love is for everyone, beauty is everywhere and living free is the only way we were meant to live.

Intro

This book is life.

There is no discrimination to age, sex, or race.

You will transcend with emotions.

There will be a time when much of life is relatable. I have gone through it and you will know someone who has too.

This book will walk you through the inevitable metaphysics of life.

There is a bit of everything for everyone in this little treasure.

Enjoy.

Progressive Frequency

Intro..*iii*

Love Thyself.. *1*

#GoodVibes *23*

Soul Connections *39*

Love Thyself

Today I woke up and decided to press play.

No more pausing, waiting or unnecessary delay.

I've accepted I can't go back to fix and rewind.

I don't want to relive or fast forward time.

I'll grow from the lessons bestowed upon me.

And know with full faith here is where I should be.

No questions to ask, no doubt left to fill.

I'll remain on my task of peace and freewill.

I awoke from the slumber, with intentions to dive.

In all the discomfort, we run from and hide.

No malice, no judgement, no hatred no pride.

No ego, no torture no place for this to reside.

Farewell to the creature who had not one clue.

Hello to this beautiful soul, it's way overdue.

We spend the first half of our lives learning how to obey rules and what's expected of us. Some of us break free from expectations and spend the next half exploring life on our terms, realigning with our purpose, finding our passions. Others aren't as lucky forcing the universe to push us into directions turned into lessons, heartbreaks and tears- living the true definition of insanity until we finally get it. I've been there; in the ugliest, darkest, coldest, loneliest places thinking I deserved it every time, ready to surrender into a deeper hell. Something happened one day...I snatched up the storm in formation and flipped it upside down. I embraced my tears and was happy I could love so hard. I felt my heart aching in pain and told myself- this will pass. I knew I had been here before but this time felt different, I had the power to control how deep I wanted to fall. Emotional pain lasts a few minutes and anything after that is the energy we are giving it to keep it alive. What about giving that energy back to source (yourself) and keeping you alive?

Love yourself.

I'm sorry for torturing you with the most negative thoughts in every situation.

I'm sorry for keeping you sheltered.

I'm sorry for downplaying your intelligence to make others feel better.

I'm sorry for not taking care of you.

I'm sorry for abusing your heart.

I'm sorry for turning my back on you.

I'm sorry for not loving you.

I'm sorry for never thinking you were good enough.

I'm sorry for allowing you to think your life was worthless.

I'm sorry for allowing anyone to dictate your feelings.

I'm sorry for being your enemy.

I'm sorry for not letting you grow.

I'm sorry for hurting you.

I'm sorry for not being your friend.

I'm sorry I didn't inspire you with creativity.

I'm sorry for not letting us live.

I've been working on loving myself to a capacity where no one can infiltrate, manipulate or influence who I am. I used to have this wall up when I met people, letting them in layer by layer until I didn't recognize who I was anymore. My energy was heavy, I was in a constant worry and I felt lost. I was right where others wanted me to be; vulnerable and unfocused. I had no voice, I felt guilty for being creative and I felt my purpose was to make others feel good...even if that meant I didn't. I made people uncomfortable in my comfort. These layers were everything that made me who I am and for mere acceptance from others, I allowed them to nip away and steal whatever they can strengthen in themselves. I was broken down to nothing until all I had left was a reflection of someone who wanted to be loved.

I began to ground myself to help protect my energy and differentiate my emotions from others, quickly realizing these burdens weren't mine to carry. In doing so, I fell so in love with who I was and started accepting who I was becoming. I found the light that so many have dimmed. People can have so much influence on us, especially if you're an empath. The best part about these energies not originating from you is THAT exactly- you don't own them, so stop allowing them to own you.

Meditate to gain clarity, listen to your intuition and decide where your loyalty stands- with your sanity, happiness and health or with toxic, negative and draining vibes? You can love people from afar, love people and not fuck with them, love people without becoming them.

Repeat "I love you, but I love myself more."

It's become a task too much to bare.

It's painfully exciting to be self-aware.

I'm done listening to lies I pretend to believe.

I'm not that oblivious and far from naïve.

It's a struggle to remain silent when the garbage that's shared sounds like whimsical knowledge to others' ears.

There's a thin line that will never have full balance when you are awake; you either remain a little warm hearted or completely desolate.

I am struggling to shift myself into the perfect equation that eliminates frustration and enhances my vibration.

Forever chasing intoxicating revelations to feed this high and increase my elevation.

Listen to that inner whisper; those puzzling words that softly echo in your head. The ones that tend to go ignored. We hear them over and over…

"This isn't good for you…. this isn't right…. that's not the truth…. you know better…that was odd…" Engage in those feelings that surface; the comfort, the hurt the love or the pain. Our true self knows when something is wrong. It is our physical body that fights this awareness. We become the complex human that can't feel and think simultaneously so we diminish one trait to enhance the other.

But we know.

We know within the first few moments what energies will elevate our vibes and which ones will deceive it. We are aware of betrayal when action is nothing more than a transparent seed. We are in love's forecast when comfort sings and vulnerability tickles.

Yet we fight both.

We inadvertently confuse the two and redefine a thief of hearts for an eloquent charmer. Sometimes it's as if the universe wants to send a reminder of these vibrational forces that weave into our aura with synchronicities.

And still, we fail to listen.

Until our hearts are pierced, we disengage with all the answers within our soul.

Wishing farewell in full certainty to an old and vaguely acquainted part of my story...and fearlessly welcoming all the unfamiliar serene specs of life waiting to latch onto me.

People aren't ready for the truth. They want a raw form of emotions but are incapable to reciprocate the vulnerability that comes with being honest. We have been cursed to coexist with unemotional creatures, lingering around indestructible barriers, searching for an ethereal entity that will ignite something within us. The truthful ones are constantly crushed and disappointed with the trust they instill in the wrong souls. But what do we do when that's all that surrounds us? What do we do when wounded hearts are patched with bullshit mediocracy? And the simplicity of remaining unattached, selfishly loving themselves? These leeches scream, "Love me! love me!" and run with a spark of light expecting to stay bright enough to feed one of their own.

Invest in your vibe.

Constrict your energy.

Remain aware.

Keep your chakras balanced.

Reinvent your roots.

Free your heart.

Brighten your aura.

Forgive, forget, move on.

Embrace the unfamiliar.

Indulge in nature.

Respect your vibrations.

Wander the wonders.

The sun will never experience darkness. Regardless of the duality that is presented in this world or the laws that the universe has provided, where dark meets light and bad meets good, the sun is the essence of all Life.

I remember what it was like when stress consumed me. Endless thoughts of every scenario possible...I saw no ending to the situation. Stubbornly, I'd disengage with the world because I was a shameful failure yet again. I'd whisper for help while I drowned in tears. Having the universe say "NO, not this way and Hell noooo" to everything I wanted. There's always a bigger picture and reason to why we are redirected in ways that make us feel something. I started to listen when I was in my feelings, anger uprooted, or hurt. I stopped and asked myself:

"What is this teaching me? What is this answering?"

I was so worked up on how things are supposed to be, trying to replicate the image in my head. Again, I questioned:

"Why am I dragging this out? What purpose does this really have in my life?"

I made the choice to grow. I trust the universe is guiding me in the direction of my soul's purpose, eliminating chaos in the way and freeing me from things I can't control.

– Stop. Relax. Breathe. A minor panic of solitude drifted past me, but I felt loved.

I still cried, but I was breathing.

Stress is not welcomed here. It is a temporary obstacle needed to shift me out of my comfort zone, appreciate my blessings and work on my flaws. I look forward to the day stress comes to visit and I gracefully roll the fucker off my shoulders.

Energies don't have laws on distance. You can easily think about something so much, feed power, vibrate energy and manifest an environment of thoughtful intentions; with no regards to frequencies (can be positive or negative). You can literally project your feelings and emotions onto anyone in the world. Empaths suffer greatly if they aren't grounded and aware of their vulnerable spirit; they can become confused and act irrationally. In short: It is very possible to know someone (intentions, flaws, fears, humility, etc...) without them ever saying a word to you. Before surfacing, vibrations "om" quite a beat...

There's this light within you waiting to be discovered. Waiting to wake up. Waiting to ignite and set your soul on fire. That healing, love, growth or misconceived external connection has always been within. All the power is within. We dim our lights so others can shine, we hide our truths, lose sight of our passions and blindly search for more. You need to completely embody the person you want to be. Mindset, habits, SELF TALK, people, energies, surroundings- all that comes into work. How are you going to have space for what you want if you're still carrying what you don't? You can learn a million different ways to better yourself but it won't help you until you intentionally apply these lessons. Expecting light without honoring your dark, love without understanding your demons or growth without change is not practical. There are so many dreamers out there... people content with thinking and hoping about a life they put no effort into manifesting because the talk of it was exciting enough. They are literally drained from living a toxic life...but wake up every day fighting the alignment that is triggering them. Those triggers are screams for change, not comfort in who you are. It takes 3 weeks to break a habit and pick up a new one. Every 21 days you have a chance to reinvent yourself, every day you have a choice to start over.

Turn on the light. Tune in!

No matter how much you want to see the good in someone, you also need to feel the good in them. There are plenty people out there ready to give you the love and support you deserve, don't sell yourself short chasing people who don't want to be bothered. I often see the best in people and hold onto it tightly after every setback. If you find yourself missing major elements of what a friendship should feel like, it's time to reclaim your power and let them go. If you conformed yourself to the comfort of others every time someone said you were too much, you would not be living your truth.

You would not be happy.

You wouldn't strive for better.

You wouldn't have a vision and your passion would be nonexistent.

Building discernment to know when to let go is everything. Growth looks different for everyone. Growth feels different for everyone. Growth is different for everyone. People come along our paths to help guide us on our journey, not every single person is meant to tag along. As heavy as it can be to let go of someone, it's not your burden to carry. It's much lighter (lit!) to move on. When you start living your truth, you will grow at an immense speed without hesitation..it gets easier. Your life depends on you.
Let's grow!

Learning to dis-empower ego is no joke. When ego is in the driver seat, you accept things as they feel and not as they are. For everything in life, if you subtract ego- you get the full experience for what it's meant to be. Ego decides if the experience is good or if it's bad. If I allow my feelings to get worked up in anger, frustration or any low vibed emotions, I'm powering more of that energy to come back to me. These things happen because ego was hurt, control wasn't in my favor. If we were meant to control every aspect in life, how stressed out would we be when obstacles arise? Is it worth the drainage and yelling? Did we get to fully experience and remain present in the moment or does memory recall you frantic? Is it really a win for you or your ego? Like damn, does all this energy worked up even feel right anymore? You can have a sense of control over what you want out of life by switching gears inside and mediating on it, creating a positive energy source to release and trust that your wishes have been heard. Trust your life will play out as it's meant to. And that stupid saying, only dead fish go with the flow is very ego driven. Going with the flow of life is much more intricate than these words, as with anything- it starts within. If you are connected with your inner being, grounded, aware and practicing whichever form of meditation feels right to you- you will go with the flow by default and trust it entirely. You cannot go with the flow without working within. You cannot release ego without working on reclaiming the power to grow from within.

When you look ahead at what's to come, it can be overwhelming. Not knowing where you're going, or knowing where and having to leave some things or people behind. We don't choose when we are born or when we pass but we are part of the co-creation in between. Lots of us just stay in limbo and the want of something is enough for them. I am constantly visiting other worlds of "what if" - expanding my own reality. Taking action to manifest the future I know I deserve is my choice alone. Doing nothing is a burden I don't want to carry. Everything new is always coated with fear but once it's greeted with acceptance, layers quickly start to fall off so the beauty of change is welcomed.

It's all perspective.

You know what's important for self-love, growth, and enlightenment??

All the "re's" in life.

Reflect- Being around people that bring out the best in you yes, but sometimes being around people that bring out the REFLECTion in you.

Recharge- Recharging as many times a day as you need to. Taking time to honor, balance and ground yourself.

Reject- Rejecting old patterns, rejecting toxic thoughts, rejecting anything that doesn't serve your highest self.

Reset- Resetting and starting over as many times as it feels right to you. There is no one way to get there, everyone's journey has to be different. Embrace yours.

Rejoice- Taking time to rejoice and be grateful for where you are right now. Gracefully progressing to each level while appreciating the last will remind you how far you've come and how unlimited your elevation can be.

Reprogram- Taking that step to reprogram the way you think, speak, process and act will open perspectives that may resonate with you.

Realign- You don't have to take everything in. You don't have to practice something that no longer serves you. You are growing everyday even if there isn't something significant that comes out of each day. You have to take time to revisit your beliefs, goals, patterns, and passions to determine what needs to be realigned. Because you will have off days that will feel like you took 10 steps back when really that's just resistance taking you somewhere you need to strengthen.

REST- We can be so hard on ourselves. If we don't take the time to rest our minds and bodies, we can't go forward. Period.

I think it's important to know when reflections are triggers and when they aren't. In a perfect world, every single encounter can be perceived as a mirror of our inner selves, things we love and hate most, and mainly things we need to work on. But sometimes...people are just plain shitty. And you don't have to tie yourself up with their growth process. It takes an abundance of discernment to separate what is a growing lesson for yourself, and what isn't. Don't pick yourself apart to the point of feeling defeated over troubled souls. There are so many reasons why people act the way they do and not every time does it call for insight on your end. Sometimes we just need to be grateful we can see past this moment, sometimes it's an opportunity to show compassion and just listen, to teach, talk, be there, spread joy/light/love, sometimes it's the universe saying I need you to handle this because I know you can..20 times in a row. Maybe we need to master certain demons. Maybe we need to be reminded of who we aren't anymore and it may be time to shift our surroundings. If you feel calm, submissive and somewhat comfortable during a trigger, it's not your burden to hold. I do know that if you truly feel grounded on one level and suddenly are uprooted it's not always an inner lesson to tear yourself apart. It's a worldly lesson to shine your fuckin light.

The same light that lit my way this far, I'm hoping on my worst days I won't forget how magical I am.

#GoodVibes

Brave heart, you got this, don't give in to those fears.

Release the grip, unclench your fist and smile through the tears.

It's never easy growing, changing, recreating your ways.

Chasing what aligns within you will bring the peace you endlessly crave.

Brave heart you've come so far to give up and turn around.

There's no limit to what you can do when your soul is unbound.

No set of rules can hold you back from your calling and true purpose.

It's up to you to push on through and how much you believe you deserve this.

You hold the power, you have the force, you can lean all the way in.

Every lesson you reflect and master will transmute into a win.

You decide how deep you go, when you are ready, how high you soar.

Honor your universal light, the true essence of your core.

Brave heart, you live for you.

You have to always speak it into existence. Tell yourself every day, "I got this. It's going to get better," and it will. If you think an ounce of negativity you will receive 5 pounds in return. Even when you see NO way and feel crazy to think there is one, that's OK…be crazy. Have faith but control your thoughts and the words you speak because words become action. Manifestation is magic. Your words are spells. Be conscious with the words you say. Emotional highs and lows should never dictate your words, if they do you will send mixed signals to the universe and receive ups and downs in life.

We are so caught up in our own image of what we think life is like that we dismiss the simple and obvious certainties. We dismiss angels with messages as nosey opinionated people. We dismiss signs and obstacles as burdens placed to specifically make your path challenging, but most of all we dismiss ourselves of what we truly deserve. We dismiss our instincts about that person we know is wrong but feels so right. We dismiss our talents to be mediocre when they are unique and amazing. We dismiss people, great fuckin souls with dope ass vibes, because of this one-eyed visualization. Dismissal of a broader vision is nothing less than a dismissal of the life that's truly meant for you.

Sometimes we receive that change we are searching for in a form we aren't ready to accept. Many times we ask for some kind of sign but ignore the ones that continue to surface. Change is a natural, fundamental process which is essential for us to accept in order to continue evolving in a world that doesn't stop transforming. Decline the blessings filled with doubt, disguised as fear and watch the lessons you will create to acknowledge the changes that need to be made.

Strip yourself from your ego that is holding you back.

Forget about all the trophies you feel you lack.

Say bye to your pride that keeps you fighting inside

from the person you are but instead you choose to hide.

Jump off the ivory tower of selfish conceptions.

Stop adding bricks to your mindless deceptions.

Pay no mind to judgement or critical beings.

Your soul is to be lived in dimensions where words have no meaning.

Let go of the life you structured in your head and

live the moment you've been blessed with instead.

Stop fearing, stop doubting to fight it or lose it.

You've been given a chance to be you so just use it.

Open your mind, create space for peace to live

Let go of all the hurt and recklessly forgive.

A potion for freedom, happiness and clarity

Now hold my hand, don't let go and believe.

Blooming through bursts of expansion.

Transitioning fear into power.

Taking each day as it comes, releasing each moment as it passes.

Being here, appreciating creation.

Growing as I humbly bloom to the next level.

Be inspired, not intimidated. Negativity will latch onto something that could've been beneficial, deceivingly altering the result. Did you know you can take any toxic emotion and (with practice) channel it into something positive?? Don't let situations, people or ideas intimidate you- intimidation only instills doubt and fear, holding you back from vibrating at a higher frequency and manifesting your true intentions. Intimidation acts as a blindfold, paralyzing our authenticity. Not only do we have the ability to create positive outcomes with optimistic thoughts, we can also change the energy of an occurrence that left us a little shattered and torn. A break up can be reconstructed into a beautiful love story by switching a few words around and appreciating the lessons instead of speaking about it negatively.

It's the power of words; words in our thoughts, the words we choose to repeat, the words we read and words we hear. Words are tagged with a bundle of emotions that subconsciously dictate our perception of everything connected to us. Use only words you would like to become and you will see how there is beauty in every day.

She got lost in a world of hope.

Feeling ambivalent about everything in life.

Forever misunderstood with a character that was taken too lightly.

She is the ditz, she is clumsy and she will laugh at it all.

She learned to stay silent because people fear to learn more than what they think they know.

The urge to be correct was constantly hidden with a nod and a smile.

If only you knew.

Gently drifting away from the simplicity, she conformed to.

She spoke less and was heard more.

Dreams became a rough draft to her reality of a masterpiece.

Expressing her most valuable guidance within her.

Without words.

Manipulating the thought process; placing action before announcement.

Bonding hope with faith.

Because words were no longer empty when they come after a promise that didn't need to be made.

Isn't is mind-blowing that one day none of this will matter; all the hours we put into school to then commit to work to pay for us to live, all the places we go, food we eat, our favorite indulges, our thoughts, our feelings, our clothes, the never ending massive number of shoes, our look.

None of it will ever matter.

What matters is the people we meet, the impressions we leave, the hearts we touch and the ones we don't, the words we speak and write, our actions and lack thereof. Our dreams won't matter unless WE make them come true. The legacy we leave, the imprint of our smile, our beauty is all that's left. The beauty inside of us. Nothing on the outside matters. Beauty is all that remains, the beauty in our spirit.

We can't fear to love. We must detach fear from love because all we are doing is depriving ourselves from possibilities that could either bring us closer with a learning lesson or shoot us directly to what we perceive love to be. Fear is nothing more than an empty perception in an unfamiliar body. It pinches you out your element and places you above a few dimensions, hovering over your confused and doubtful soul.

Still, we fear...

Most barriers stem from our egos, expectations and greed. Think about all the things we unintentionally hold ourselves back from because of the cluttered teachings that have been drilled into our minds. We've been programmed to take as many detours we have to, as long as we get there. That's such BS. You know that job is stressful, you know that friend is fake, you know that person is toxic...yet you keep hoping for change, cashing in on the highest currency you won't get back- your time. You don't have to live life according to programmed expectations!!

Being unhappy creates conflict.

Being unbalanced creates conflict.

Living a life not aligned to your purpose or that doesn't resonate within you IS conflict.

It's conflicting with your core beliefs, your soul urge and human experience. We create 99% of our own problems. Change your perspective, look for blessings instead of closed doors. Say NO when your vibes tell you to. Love yourself and there will be no room for troubles to disturb your peace. Get out of your way. Sadness, anger, disappointments -
are emotions that come and go.

Trust your intuition, feel the vibes, let the universe guide you.

I need to rid myself of empathy.

It destroys my mental clarity.

I have been cursed with the tendency

To heal and love consistently,

To kiss tears that fall effortlessly

And warm your heart with felicity.

I am my biggest fan. I silently repeat positive affirmations to myself. I tell myself I am beautiful. I stop and place my hand on my chest to feel my heartbeat. I remind myself I am enough. I dress in clothes that I feel comfortable in and play with the infinite color palettes of makeup. I pause and look in the mirror to admire my unique features. I play with my hair, read, write and take walks…alone. I feel good. I am happy. I am free and at peace. I work hard and challenge myself. I never stop learning.

We linger around waiting to meet a lost soul, in hopes they can validate our existence and enhance the love we have for ourselves. Nobody can ever love you more than you can love you and you don't need anyone to dictate how much or how little love you deserve. I am my best friend and if you aren't fighting to win that kind of love I am better off loving myself alone.

Why do you feel rejected? What expectations have you set in order for rejection to be invited? Having expectations can be your own blinding rejection. You can have decent moral standards and boundaries with no expectations. What you accept has nothing to do with what you expect. How silly is it to get mad at someone, hold grudges and break friendships because we expect a certain behavior from them- that sounds very controlling. Instead, try releasing your expectations and you will strip the power from rejection. If the same people (or circumstances) keep making you feel devalued, release the expectations you set for them, accept and love them for who they are- not what you expect them to be. Harness your energy. There is nothing you can miss out that won't present itself to you again, if you are meant to have it. So whether its friends, events, gifts or just the word NO, accept that as the universe guiding you. Be your own preference, put yourself first and take time to connect with your inner being. You don't have to be the loudest, prettiest, funniest, richest, fittest or smartest to be accepted by you. Your self-worth isn't measured by the validation from others but by the acceptance of yourself. .

Soul Connections

Bitter

You fell in love with me because I was naïve to the world.

I am the woman you molded from a little girl.

You took advantage of my vulnerability, my young mind and spirit.

You soaked it all up making it impossible for anyone to get near it.

You became disturbed, compulsive and conniving.

There was a devil in you, there sure was no denying.

You went from the man I love and the one I adore,

To the one I hate and didn't know anymore.

I went from loving you to thinking you were a King.

Slowly with your actions you shattered my dreams.

You destroyed my space, my home and my love.

I had no dignity left, you took everything you could think of.

...

Sweet

There was a day a girl met a boy.

She fell so in love, completely overjoyed.

Nothing else mattered, it was all irrelevant.

If it didn't have you involved it never made sense.

Her dreams and reality were never balanced.

She waited for the day you would comprehend.

You were her world, her meaning her life.

She envisioned the day she would become your wife.

You took for granted, the woman she became.

You could not balance love and your foolish games.

In the end you won, your wishes came true.

But what's you without her, what's she without you?

There will always be questions, you gave up too soon.

That's the game of love, the trophy of a fool.

My life was a blur till you came along.

You brought purpose and love to a sad boring song.

I will never forget you or even try.

It's like saying hello without a goodbye.

I love you, I'll never regret.

What I am to you, I hope you never forget.

You teased me with the words you said, I thought you'd always be here.

But when I look around and need you most, you are nowhere near.

Where have you gone?

You just up and left me all alone,

In this world, so big and so cold.

Now I'm left with no one to hold.

I knew it was too good to be true.

Some things in life are just not meant for you.

These layers, this wall you tore down…you promised you'd be around.

Naked I lie here and stare into space

These thoughts I can't bear, your image can't be erased.

I shouldn't fight it, should just leave it and let it fade away.

I can't deny it, thought I needed you for all my days.

Let the memory fade, I'll wait for it.

You're my biggest mistake, my heart paid for it.

She will always wander off and search for stories lost in a silent stare.

She'll seem odd as she smiles and continues on her path.

If she can't grow with you...you'll become a chapter in her book, a lesson in her life and a love story in her gaze.

They really will pretend to be an entire different human. They'll have you fooled into thinking they're vibrating on the same frequency and hold conversations that make your soul want it all. You give in completely only to come back out with guilt, shame and hurt because your perfect human wasn't them. Don't let the greedy soul snatchers taint your beautiful vibe. Keep loving hard, thinking big and exploring the world with an innocent heart and vibrant mind. Keep being you. No guards, no walls, no expectations.

Give love to show love and you will become love.

The Beginning of the End

We started out the way everyone does, never knowing it would grow into love.

Blissfully happy and worry free, never doubting we were meant to be.

Outings and gifts, all the good stuff…but within time it got real tough.

Yelling and screaming, anger and fights…sad and lonely, very cold nights.

Tears are seen, and hearts are broken. Promises become meaningless as hurtful words are spoken.

Slowly but surely, we are being torn apart. Sadness and bitter confusion crept into our hearts.

A couple years later we're barely friends. How I wish I knew it was the beginning of the end.

Angel Touch

I prayed and asked God to give me strength and love.

Never did I imagine that my angel was listening from up above.

My angel came to me when I was sleeping, and showed me many things,

But I found it very awkward to see my angel had no wings.

My angel had no voice, nor a visible face.

But my angel did give me strength and love nobody could replace.

My angel had a touch I would never forget.

A touch that set me free and made everything perfect.

When I awoke my angel wasn't there.

My angel must've done its job then disappeared.

I still feel that touch in everything I do,

But I only feel it most whenever I'm with you.

I literally ripped my heart and guts out and handed it all to the devil himself.

He was an angel in sober moments, a monster intoxicated.

He killed every part of what makes me who I am every day.

But I still stood.

Fear is a bitch I don't ever want to reacquaint myself with.

I want everything you're not.

I had to walk through hell alone to find my heavenly home.

Most of love is lost in the words we do not share.

I tried to fight every temptation.

Your silly texts were not wanted here, but wait…you made me smile.

Don't hug me like that---feeling your body against mine sent me chills that I'm not supposed to feel with you.

Why are you staring at me?

You really think I'm beautiful?

This isn't a date, don't open that door for me.

Why is your laugh so contagious? Why did I feel vulnerable?

I want to pinch you for being so sweet to me.

This can't be real.

I don't remember the last time I laughed so much.

You could be so perfect for me.

What am I thinking?

I don't want to leave, let's just talk and things.

We shouldn't be doing this. I feel so weak in your arms.

I never felt more perfect than the moments I'm with you.

I tasted Earth in your kiss.

Orgasmic paradise.

Our moments are everything.

I guess with love, there are no rules.

But I will never tell you….

Only our insides will know the love that we hold so deep within our hearts for each other. Maybe a love so imperfectly real it causes endless destruction when we try to indulge in it. Emotions I had to repair started to burst from beneath the wounds that were now covered with specs of stardust. Memories recreated in my head all with a repetitive ending of uncertainty for what to expect next. Holding tight to the cord not remembering where it all began and searching to find no end. Lost, afraid, vulnerable and defeated. Comfort at its worst but too contempt to question it. Forgetting this isn't what love is about.

You've exhausted your chances.

Took my heart on too many dances.

You left my soul in a frenzy of trances.

This is nothing romantic.

A story of conflicting glances.

Let's avoid the mess, remain emotionless

Escape the stress, no love to profess.

Selfishness we express, as feelings digress.

Watch our souls transgress to a realm too complex.

She Left him.

She just couldn't do it anymore. Waking up every day, never feeling fully rested. Her mind obsessively running with frantic thoughts of what could always go wrong. There was no spark in her heart, butterflies in her stomach or life in her eyes. Love consumed her soul but this was no longer love. What was once a captivating voyage recklessly turned into dust leaving no desire to participate in life. She felt defeated. Fear was pumping through her veins and feeling lost was routine.

She woke up

And ran.

I'm fighting the fall,

Scared to give you my all.

It's getting harder to hide,

The feelings I'm keeping inside.

Can't let go, grip is too strong,

But I know with love, we will never go wrong.

I need to be brave,

flee the passions I've encaged.

This was the race,

I had chosen to chase.

Restricted to preserve the essence of my light.

Close my eyes shut as I prepare my body to take flight.

That feeling when you want to see someone from your past just to catch up on life…everything they missed out on, share how much you both have grown. You imagine how proud they will be to know those dreams you shared you are now living, how everything changed for the better, and the only thing that remains the same is their absence. Missing them never goes away because they were supposed to be right by your side to celebrate life with you. I won't understand how a final goodbye is what it takes to welcome the new world that's waiting to bless you with dreams that were once shared with someone you lost.

Embracing the pain

Is what I need to gain

The clarity to maintain

The love that now stains

Every part of my brain

Embracing the pain

Is the only way

To deal with the days

I'm here left to face

Alone and misplaced

In this erratic race

Don't ask me to put my walls down when you have no intention on being on the other side ready to let go of all your inhibitions as well. Don't ask me to love you when you can't love yourself enough to realize something genuinely good for your soul. Don't ask me to be true when you disguise your emotions with the outside world. I'm tired of people coming into my world, running with my heart to fix a soulless pawn.

I'm not supposed to love you, I'm not supposed to care.

I shouldn't fall asleep at night wishing you were here.

I'm yearning for your touch, craving for your kiss.

You feed my body with formidable lust, and fill my heart with sheer bliss

With every perfect night of this forbidden love we share,

You release the tension in my soul, I'm as free as air.

I get lost in your gaze, feel intensely hot inside.

My mind is a maze, an uncontrollable tide.

I'm high on sex, intoxicated with affection.

Under your spell I'm perplexed, loves' most dangerous perception.

I wish you fought like I meant something.

Your heart was cold, tired and forever numbing.

I should've seen all these years stream through your tears.

The day I decided to walk away you didn't hesitate or convince me to stay.

You let me be, set me free understood it wasn't you but was me.

You said people change and they grow, you had been here before so you know.

I cried inside, silenced my heart and mind.

I couldn't tell if you were pretending you were really at peace with us ending.

I wish I could've heard your pain to know love for me in your heart still remains.

I released the pen, you closed the chapter.

There was no love to chase or go after.

I feel safe and secure, I don't want nothing more than to love you.

You are home and I know just how far we will go when I love you.

Energies we will match, cosmic highs we will catch because I love you.

Growing in, breathing out, lighting our world around because
our loves' true.

You've been my biggest reflection; it's not about building perfection, but love is the lesson... I never want to be less than.

You woke up something inside of me, the rest of the world was too scared to see. My light now shines so brightly, as I float in high vibrancy.

It's been real in your arms, all the feels in your charm when you love me.

Skipping beats in my heart, butterflies from the start because you love me.

Waking up, tearing down all the ties that were bound when you love me.

Being one in our soul, sharing all that we know because our loves' free.

www.ingramcontent.com/pod-product-compliance
Lightning Source LLC
Chambersburg PA
CBHW071319080526
44587CB00018B/3286